MW01280287

This
Becoming Journal
belongs to

beginning date

Copyright © 2005 by J. Countryman

Published by the J. Countryman® division of the Thomas Nelson
Book Group., Nashville, Tennessee 37214

All rights reserved. No portion of this publication may be
reproduced, stored in a retrieval system or transmitted in any
form by any means—except for brief quotations in printed
reviews—without the prior written permission of the publisher.

J. Countryman® is a trademark of Thomas Nelson, Inc.

New Century Version®. Copyright © 1987, 1988, 1991 by
Thomas Nelson, Inc. All rights reserved. Used by permission.

Design: Koechel Peterson & Associates I Minneapolis, Minnesota

Project Editor: Kathy Baker

ISBN 1 4041

Printed and bound in the United States of America

www.thomasnelson.com I www.jcountryman.com

becoming

Journal

NCV

Nashville, Tennessee

Charm can fool you,

and beauty can trick you,

but a woman

who respects the Lord

should be praised.

proverbs 31:30

We women are on a constant journey of Becoming.

Becoming wiser as we mature

Becoming more involved in others' lives

Becoming more influential in our communities

Becoming better friends, daughters, wives, mothers, sisters

Becoming more immersed in the will of God

We're also Becoming . . .

Less satisfied with the ideals of this world

Less entranced by the things of this world

Less likely to fall for the lies of this world

Or at least we aspire to Become all those things.

Let this journal be an encouraging companion
along your own journey of Becoming.

Making a Change

John said, "Change your hearts and lives because the kingdom of heaven is near."
MATTHEW 3:2

Tues 9/16   Being ignored - which I know is
            what's best although it makes me
            very sad.

no
laughs   3 soccer games
            Not home - Ron Kahle Sr.   bed
                                        alone

Weds 9/17   CCD class was good; work
            was productive - need to
            look into Rothonville or similar
no
laughs   Beers w/ Rick

Sat 10/4

Came home to a
party. Greg was
having a great time
w/out me

We're always changing, Becoming different in big or subtle ways. Part of being women of God is to manage those changes, to make sure our hearts and lives are more and more in tune with the kingdom of God. With that in mind, what do you need to change?

Sun 10/5

I chose to be loving instead
of being a bitch — cleaned
up the mess and offered to
get him coffee.

He chose not to go golfing
with us — again.

"Those who do
right more than
anything else are
happy, because
God will fully
satisfy them."

MATTHEW 5:6

The Healthiest Diet

Jesus answered, "It is written in the scriptures, 'A person doesn't live by eating only bread, but by everything God says'."

MATTHEW 4:4

There's more to
nourishment than
balancing your
carbohydrates, fats, and
proteins. You need to
feast on God's word.
How's your diet going?

"Those people who keep their faith until the end will be saved. The Good News about God's kingdom will be preached in all the world, to every nation. Then the end will come."

MATTHEW 24:13, 14

More than Words

So you're not so good with words. You get all tongue-tied when you're trying to say what's on your heart. Or maybe you have a natural way with words. Either way, it doesn't matter when it comes to prayer, because God isn't looking for grand or flowery words. The Lord wants to have simple, honest conversation with you. Don't let your words—for good or bad—get in the way. Say what's on your heart. Write what is on your heart right now.

When you pray,
don't be like
those people who
don't know God.
They continue
saying things that
mean nothing,
thinking that God
will hear them
because of their
many words.

MATTHEW 6:7

"Don't judge other people, or you will be judged. You will be judged in the same way the you judge others, and the amount you give to others will be given to you."

MATTHEW 7:1, 2

becoming

Less is More

The race is on, and the winner is the one who dies with the most "stuff!" We exhaust ourselves in a mad dash to acquire the biggest, the best, the most. We have confused our wants with our needs.

Stop the madness! Remember the old saying, "Less is more?" Simplify your life. Are you guilty of chasing after more stuff than you really need? What things do you need to get rid of to simplify life?

*"Your Father
knows the things
you need before
you ask him."*

becoming

"Keep your lives
free from
the love of money,
and be satisfied
with what you have."

HEBREWS 13:5

"YOU SHOULD BE A
LIGHT FOR OTHER
PEOPLE, LIVE SO
THAT THEY WILL SEE
THE GOOD THINGS
YOU DO AND WILL
PRAISE YOUR FATHER
IN HEAVEN."

GIVE IT A REST

"Come to me,
all of you who are tired
and have heavy loads,
and I will give you rest."

Matthew 11:28

The heaviness of worry can weigh us down and wear us out in no time! But Jesus knows and understands the burdens we carry. When we give him our heaviest struggles, he will rejuvenate our spirits and set our minds at ease. What burdens do you need to release today? Can you let him give you rest?

becoming

"If you believe,

you will get

anything you ask for

in prayer."

MATTHEW 21:22

"Listen, I am sending you out like sheep among wolves.
So be as smart as snakes and as innocent as doves."

MATTHEW 10:16

becoming

Eden is Becoming more
polluted and dangerous by
the minute. We have to be
hard and mean and maybe
even a little bit dirty to
survive, right? Not so. Jesus
told us to be different—
to be gentle and innocent.
Can you trust the Lamb
enough to Become a strong,
smart sheep like him?

"Whoever is not with me
is against me.
Whoever does not work with me
is working against me."

MATTHEW 12:30

becoming

A Secret Worth Telling

"You have been chosen to know the secrets about the kingdom of heaven."

MATTHEW 13:11

becoming

"Your Father
can see what is
done in secret,
and he will
reward you."

MATTHEW 6:4

Do you have any secrets? Of course you do.
But God knows what you're hiding—good and bad—and he loves you.
He's watching you not to catch you in the act of messing up,
but to see the good things and reward you for them.
He wants to make your life better and better.
God also has secrets, and like a true best friend,
he's sharing them with you. Open his diary, the Bible, and see.

Ask... Search... Knock

This promise is so reassuring of God's provision and care. But look a little closer. Good things happen for you, but you have to act first. "Ask...Search...Knock." Are you expecting to find something without searching for it? Are you waiting for a door to open when you haven't knocked on it? Have you forgotten to ask God for anything? And have you thanked him yet, even if the gift hasn't quite arrived?

A PIG OR A PRINCE?

Have you ever befriended a
pig or a dog? These people
don't appreciate you or they
tear you down. Eventually,
you just have to pick up your
pearls and move on! Leave
the pigs to their mud while
you go find a jeweler. What
species are you hanging out
with? If you married a pig,
how can you help the King
transform him into a prince?

*"Don't give
holy things
to dogs, and
don't throw
your pearls
before pigs.
Pigs will
only trample
on them,
and dogs will
turn to attack
you."*

becoming

Redeeming Eve

It's easy to dislike Eve. If she hadn't
messed up, everything would still be
perfect. But Eve is actually the ultimate
example of what God's grace looks like.
She was disobedient, but God still loved
her—because that's the way God is. He
loves us despite our obvious flaws and
willful disobedience. And because of this
love, Eve's relationship with God was
restored (see Genesis 4). He began a new
thing in her life, even after she failed. He
can do the same for you, too.

Here Comes the Bride

The church should be the most dynamic, life-giving, life-filled, creative organization on earth. As daughters of the King, we should love what God loves… and he loves his church! Jacob had an amazing encounter with God, and the place this occurred was the "house of God… the gate of heaven" (Genesis 28:17). There is nothing sacred about a building; a place becomes the house of God when his children are there. Jesus is committed to seeing the church fulfill its potential on earth. When you love the church, you don't treat it casually. Let the church become family. Don't just show up; participate, contribute, and do your part in helping it Become a great place to worship the King of heaven.

BE THE HERO

Did you know that you are a hero to someone? Perhaps it's your daughter, or a child in your Sunday school class, or a niece or nephew. But somewhere, a young person is looking to you for direction. The Bible has some powerful words about mentoring: "Whoever accepts a child in my name accepts me. If one of these little children believes in me, and someone causes them to sin, it would be better for that person to have a large stone tied around the neck and be drowned in the sea" (Matthew 18:5, 6). Whether or not you are a parent, you must take your role in the life of others seriously and always be aware of the example you are setting.

Becoming One

Marriage means two are Becoming one. It's a process that is announced at a wedding…and is still ongoing fifty years later. Sometimes the process is beautiful, sometimes it's painful. Think about it this way: When two plants are grafted together, part of each plant is removed, then their broken places are squeezed together until they grow together. But with patience and care, the two will Become one. When you feel pain or squeezing in your relationship, it's part of your grafting process. Give your relationship the care and patience it needs, and something beautiful and strong will emerge.

"When God made the world, 'he made them male and female.' And God said, 'So a man will leave his father and mother and be united with his wife, and the two will become one body.' So there are not two, but one. God has joined the two together, so no one should separate them."

MATTHEW 19:4-6

HOPE, HEALING, ACCEPTANCE

Marriage isn't easy. But just as Christians can never be separated from Christ's vow of love (Romans 8:38, 39), so God intends that a husband and wife not be separated from their marital vows. God may hate divorce (Malachi 2:16), but he doesn't hate divorced people. In his unfailing love, he forgives the sin of the sincerely repentant. He heals the wounds and gives hope for a restored future. We must take a stand against the rash of divorce in our culture and hold onto the hope God offers. If you're contemplating divorce, by all means get help. God absolutely delights in repairing marriages. But if yours has been irreparably broken, he will delight in repairing you.

Help Miracles Happen

We're so used to hearing that Jesus healed the blind and the crippled that we often overlook something very important. If they were blind and crippled, how did they get to Jesus in the first place? Someone had to help them. And sometimes a little help, a little faith, is all it takes to transform a life.

The blind and
crippled people
came to Jesus in
the Temple, and
he healed them.

'Love yourself'

Comparing ourselves to others can be damaging to our inner beauty. (It doesn't help our confidence either.) Jesus has a wonderful solution for this. In Matthew 22:39, he says, "Love your neighbor as you love yourself." Jesus knew we'd have a tough time loving others if we had not dealt with loving ourselves the way he made us. He wants us to stop comparing ourselves to others and see ourselves as God sees us—precious to him, his beloved children. When we begin to understand how much God loves and accepts us—just as we are—we are free to love ourselves and empowered to love others. That is the key to true inner beauty.

becoming

*Teach me
wisdom.*

*A friend loves
at all times and a
brother helps in time
of trouble.*

PROVERBS 17:17

*God says that he has
stored each one of your
tears in a bottle. God has
not turned his back on your
suffering. Even when you
feel completely alone, God
has not abandoned you. It
breaks his heart to see you
hurt. He is close enough to
catch each one of your
tears.*

You have recorded
my troubles. You
have kept a list
of my tears.

PSALM 56:8

[God] is

my defender

and my Savior,

my shield

and my protection.

PSALM 144:2

God's got your back.
Be there the next
time a friend is in
need or feels bad.
Try to do what God
would do for you.

*The Lord is kind and does what
is right...I said to myself,
"Relax, because the Lord
takes care of you."*

Whether we pray for ourselves
or others, each prayer is another
life–lesson. It gives us practice
getting on God's wavelength.
The closer we get to God's vibe,
the more we're growing.

I love the Lord, because he listens
to my prayers for help. He paid attention to me,
so I will call to him for help as long as I live.

PSALM 116:1-2

becoming

The Lord is great
and worthy of our
praise; no one can
understand how
great he is.

PSALM 145:3

Trying to handle everything on your own can turn you into a stress case who's really irritable or bossy. If you can let God step in, though, he'll team up with you. He'll help you carry the load and keep you from getting overwhelmed.

Charm can fool you and beauty can trick you,
but a woman who respects the Lord should be praised.
PROVERB 30:30

Have you ever
told a "little white
lie" that "didn't
hurt anybody" and
got you out of a
tight spot?

Some people think
they are pure, but
they are not really
free from evil.

PROVERBS 30:11

God's Word is so
reliable that you
can use it for a
shield. That's
what Jesus did
when Satan
tempted him. He
used God's words
to protect his
heart. It's good to
know that there
are not cracks in
the shield.
Everything he
says is true.

Jesus answered, "It is written . . ."

MATTHEW 4:4

Give thanks
to the Lord
because
he is good.
His love
continues
forever.

PSALM 136:1

Do you try to figure out who you are by clinging to stuff that fades? Do you get wrapped up in what you look like or what achievements you've scored? Ecclesiastes calls this "vanity." Chasing vanity leaves you hurt and back where you started.

What do people
really gain from all
the hard work they
do here on earth?

A lot of people spend all
their lives trying to get
satisfied. Cars, clothes,
tattoos, drugs—what-
ever the latest thing is
to make you feel like
somebody. New clothes
may fill you up for a few
days. And then you're
empty again. The high
doesn't last.

becoming

All the rivers flow

to the sea,

but the sea

never becomes full.

Without Jesus, this life is
all there is—no future, no
eternity to look forward to.
So when your heart is
aching, your life seems
empty, and you feel lost, go
to Jesus to be filled up and
satisfied. He will not
disappoint you.

Everything God does will continue forever.

becoming

Everything God allows in your life—
even sadness—has a purpose,
and he has worked out the timing perfectly.

There is a time for everything
and everything on earth
has its special season.

Worrying that we are not good enough
because we don't look a certain way is
a struggle. Learning to focus more on
who we are as people is worth the
effort. Lacking self–confidence can
hold us back.

becoming

*I realized the reason
people work hard and
try to succeed; They are
jealous of each other.
This, too, is useless, like
chasing the wind.*

ECCLESIASTES 4:4

Being beautiful is about more than looks. Tell your friends how much you admire their faith, intelligence, kindness, or humor. Praise what you like about them to let them know you care.

Two people are
better than one,
because they get more
done by working
together.

ECCLESIASTES 4:9

becoming

Your words are powerful. They can encourage, inspire, comfort, or explain; or they can hurt, bite, sting, or devastate. Choose your words carefully. Count to ten before you spout off.

What you say can mean life or death.

PROVERBS 18:21

What you put into
your life now can
impact what you
get out of it later.

Wisdom makes a
person stronger than
ten leaders in a city.

You can't tell by
looking at a person
if they're a Christian.
It's in their heart.

becoming

The heart of the wise
leads to right.
ECCLESIASTES 10:2

Q: Ever have one of those
years where everything you
believe in falls apart?

A: *Yep. Changing jobs, finding
out a friend betrayed you . . .
it can make you feel like
quitting everything—
including your faith. Take one
thing at a time. Try to see if
what's wrong actually has
anything to do with your
religion. You don't have to
give up on everything in life
just because you're giving up
(or have to give up) on a few
things. Hard times can
actually help you grow closer
to God.*

When I was in
trouble, I called to
the Lord, and he
answered me.

PSALM 120:1

God has given you
every moment of
your life as a gift.

Those who wait for perfect weather will never plant seeds;
those who look at every cloud will never harvest crops.

ECCLESIASTES 11:4

Ask the Lord to restore your joy, to
give you eyes to see your purpose,
and to help you make the most of
these once–in–a–lifetime days.

Sunshine is sweet;
it is good to see
the light of day.

How do you know God is with you?

becoming

He will save you
from six troubles;
even seven troubles
will not harm you.

becoming

Only in heaven will we know how
many times God has rescued us
from harm. The list probably fills
books: family car delayed in traffic
to avoid a pileup; stuck at work but
kept from a devastating hurt. Most
of the time we walk around totally
unaware of his divine intervention.
He keeps us safe from things we
can see, and things we can't see.

The past is long
gone. Tomorrow is
a dream, and right
now is the only
moment you have
to enjoy.

*People ought to
enjoy every day
of their lives,
no matter how
long they live.*

Strong Enough to be Weak

Our culture despises weakness, suffering, and brokenness. It rewards the brave, the strong, and the best. But God's ways are not our ways. He knows that when we're "tough" we're self-reliant. And when we're self-reliant, we're not God-reliant. And that's when we really get into trouble. Brokenness is the blessing that makes us depend on God for everything.

For this reason I am
happy when I have
weaknesses, insults,
hard times, sufferings,
and all kinds of trouble
for Christ. Because when
I am weak, then I am
truly strong.

2 CORINTHIANS 12:10

"You can have forgiveness of your sins through Jesus. . . . Through Jesus everyone who believes is free from all sins."

ACTS 13:38, 39

Live in the right way, serve
God, have faith, love, patience,
and gentleness.
1 TIMOTHY 6:11

Be alert. Continue strong
in the faith. Have
courage, and be strong.
Do everything in love.
1 CORINTHIANS 16:13, 14

becoming

becoming

Truly Liberated Women

Do you carry around a guilty conscience? We
all say, do, and think things we desperately
regret. But remember this: "We have freedom
now, because Christ made us free (Galatians
5:1). Take God at his word. Forgive yourself
and in faith claim the power of Christ's
freedom from guilt.

God began doing a good work in
you, and I am sure he will continue
it until it is finished when Jesus
Christ comes again.

PHILIPPIANS 1:6

A Beautiful Body

How should a woman think about
her body? God bought us with the
sacrifice of Jesus, and he puts
within the physical body of every
believer his own Holy Spirit. We are
then his temple, the place where
he lives, so God lives through us.
God loves our imperfect bodies and
wants us to use them as tools to
advance God-centered values in a
self-centered world. So when
people see us, they see bodies that
are committed to magnifying
Christ. When we look in the mirror,
we should see the beauty of Jesus
living in us.

*I will have the courage
now, as always, to show
the greatness of Christ in
my life here on earth,
whether I live or die.*

PHILIPPIANS 1:20

becoming

*When you do things, do
not let selfishness or
pride be your guide*

PHILIPPIANS 2:3

Q: Can I really know if I'm a Christian?

A: Definitely! God's Word makes it very
clear that "If you use your mouth to say,
'Jesus is Lord,' and if you believe it in your
heart that God raised Jesus from the dead,
you will be saved" (Romans 10:9). If you
truly believe and confess your belief, you are
a daughter of God.

becoming

Closing the Gap

Does there seem to be a distance between you and God sometimes? This is a common feeling, because we tend to base our relationship with God on our performance. But God isn't like that. He calls us his friends, and his love never changes, even when we mess up. Jesus makes us right with God. God doesn't see our sin; he sees Christ's righteousness. Our feelings may fluctuate, but God's do not.

I always thank my God for you because of the grace God has given you in Christ Jesus.

1 CORINTHIANS 1:4

God's riches are very
great, and his wisdom
and knowledge have no
end! No one can explain
the things God decides
or understand his ways.

ROMANS 11:33

Live in Peace

"Do your best to live in peace with everyone" (Romans 12:18). With so many relationships, circumstances, and personalities, how can we get along with everyone? For starters, understand that you are responsible for your actions, not for someone's else's reactions. You will make mistakes and offend people, so be willing to ask forgiveness and learn from it. To "live in peace" requires respect and consideration.

becoming

Sex: Christ vs. Culture

As a society we've forgotten how to blush. The tentacles of
sexual immorality are everywhere, and Christians aren't
immune to their lure. God has created sex to be beautiful,
fulfilling, and strictly for the marriage bed (Hebrews 13:4), but
when we expose ourselves to impure images, language, and
emotions, we're prone to impure thoughts and actions. As
believers, we no longer belong to ourselves; we belong to God
and are called to use our bodies for good things. We must be
careful to give ourselves wholly to Christ, not to our culture.

These two things
cannot change:
God cannot lie
when he makes a
promise, and he
cannot lie when he
makes an oath.

HEBREWS 6:18

becoming

My dear friend, do not follow what is bad; follow what is good. The one who does good belongs to God.

3 JOHN 11

No one has ever imagined what God
has prepared for those who love him.

1 CORINTHIANS 2:9

becoming

God's word is alive and
working and is sharper than
a double-edged sword.

HEBREWS 4:12

becoming

*7 Ways to Help a Friend Going
Through a Breakup*

1. Pray for healing in her heart.
2. Be there to listen, not to give advice.
3. When she confides, keep it confidential.
4. Ask her how you can help.
5. Take her on an "escape weekend."
6. Send her funny cards.
7. Avoid setting her up for a while.

This is how God showed his love to us: he sent his one and only Son into the world so that we could have life through him.

1 JOHN 4:9

If people say, "I love God," but hate their brothers or sisters, they are liars. Those who do not love their brothers and sisters, whom they have seen, cannot love God, whom they have never seen.

1 JOHN 4:20

Name one person in
your life who is difficult
to love. Now write that
person's name and read
1 John 4:20. As an act
of worship to the God of
love, ask him to show
you a brand-new way to
love that person. Ask
him to love based on
your faith in God, not
on your feelings about
that person.

Christ came only once
and for all time at just
the right time to take
away all sin by
sacrificing himself.

HEBREWS 9:26

becoming

"Seek God's
kingdom, and all
the other things
you need will be
given to you."

LUKE 12:31

Facing Problems

Stressed out? Think a little bit of temper is justified? Remember Stephen's example. When he was dragged before the people who wanted to kill him, "all the people in the meeting were watching Stephen closely and saw that his face looked like the face of an angel" (Acts 6:15). What do people see in you when times are tough?

becoming

*"God will show his
mercy forever and ever
to those who worship
and serve him"*
Luke 1:50

"All who make themselves
great will be made humble, but
those who make themselves
humble will be made great."

LUKE 14:11

becoming

Q: What does it mean to repent?

A: To repent actually means "to turn away from"—a 180-degree turn. When Scripture speaks of repentance, it means to recognize your sin, have true remorse, and make the conscious choice to not repeat the offense and to ask forgiveness from God.

"God loved the world so much that he gave his one and only Son so that whoever believes in him may not be lost, but have eternal life."

JOHN 3:16

becoming

"I am the light of the
world. The person who
follows me will never live
in darkness but will have
the light that gives light."

*"I leave you peace;
my peace I give you.
I do not give as the
world does. So don't
let your hearts be
troubled or afraid."*

JOHN 14:27

"Whoever wants
to be the most
important must
be last of all and
servant of all."

MARK 9:35

Soul Survivor

The Bible often says Jesus was "filled with compassion" for the dying, crippled, blind, and burdened. He brought hope for the hopeless and healing for the brokenhearted. The same is true today! If your spirit has been damaged by any abuse in life, know that Jesus is filled with compassion for your suffering. "The Lord is close to the brokenhearted, and he saves those who have been crushed" (Psalm 34:18).

"I tell you the truth,
whoever hears what
I say and believes in
the One who sent
me has eternal life."

becoming

I pray that the God who gives
hope will fill you with much joy
and peace while you trust in him.

ROMANS 15:13

Be Still and Know

Meditation isn't just a mystical or new age thing. It's a coming to stillness in the mind and body. It's being still to know the Holy Spirit's presence—to simply be with God. The early Christians called this "pure prayer." Meditation, like all Christian practices, requires discipline and patience, but with each attempt to "be still and know," the silence take us deeper into the mystery of God.

*Remember, God is
the One who makes
you and us strong in
Christ. God made us
his chosen people.*

2 CORINTHIANS 1:21

New eyes to see

Want to see the world in a whole new way? Pray. Through intimate connection with God we begin to see ourselves and others the way God sees us—as his beloved children. We begin to open our hearts, our homes, our calendars, and our wallets to serve him more. Today, ask God for new vision and a new heart.

The grace of the Lord Jesus
Christ, the love of God, and
the fellowship of the Holy
Spirit be with you all. 2
CORINTHIANS 13:14

*God will strengthen you
with his own great power
so that you will not give
up when troubles come,
but you will be patient.*

COLOSSIANS 1:11

*The Lord is faithful and
will give you strength
and will protect you
from the Evil One.*

2 THESSALONIANS 3:3

Pray for rulers and
for all who have
authority so that
we can have quiet
and peaceful lives
full of worship and
respect for God.

1 TIMOTHY 2:2

'Honor your father and mother'

*You never outgrow God's command to honor your parents
(Exodus 20:12), even when you're an adult. Many families are
faced with caring for an elderly family member, and sometimes
this can cause financial and emotional hardship. But caring for
aging parents is an opportunity to return the love we have
received—from our parents and from God.*

Faith means being sure
of the things we hope
for and knowing that
something is real even
if we do not see it.

HEBREWS 11:1

You were chosen to tell
about the wonderful acts
of God, who called you out
of darkness into his
wonderful light.

becoming

The Lord
knows how to
save those who
serve him when
troubles come.

2 PETER 2:9

becoming

Live to the Fullest

Are you afraid of dying? Many
people are, but we have Christ's
assurances that we can have
peace. For those who follow
Christ, death is a mere
passageway from this life into the
next. Christ has promised you will
receive a perfect body, eternal
satisfaction, and reunion with God
forever. Christ conquered death,
so we can make the most of life.

Since these children are people
with physical bodies, Jesus
himself became like them. He
did this so that, by dying, he
could destroy the one who has
the power of death—the devil—
and free those who were like
slaves all their lives because of
their fear of death.

HEBREWS 2:14, 15

becoming

"When the Holy Spirit comes to you, you will receive power. You will be my witnesses—in Jerusalem, in all of Judea, in Samaria, and in every part of the world."

If any of you
needs wisdom,
you should ask
God for it. He
is generous and
enjoys giving
to all people, so
he will give you
wisdom.

JAMES 1:5

becoming

becoming

The Beginning

There really will be an end to the world as we know it. There really is a happily ever after with God in heaven. Both in this life and in the next God has provided abundant life beyond our imagining, but in heaven we'll have all the good without any of the bad. We'll rule with Christ, enjoy rewards, and be heirs with him. And best of all, we'll finally "get" who God is!

You were made holy,
and you were made
right with God in the
name of the Lord
Jesus Christ and in the
Spirit of our God.

1 CORINTHIANS 6:11

becoming

*"Whoever is your
servant is the greatest
among you. Whoever
makes himself great
will be made humble.
Whoever makes himself
humble will be made
great."*

MATTHEW 23:11, 12

Remember, God is
the One who makes
you and us strong
in Christ. God
made us his chosen
people.
2 CORINTHIANS 1:21

becoming

Be Trusting, Not a Pushover

Are you a pushover? If you find others taking advantage, perhaps it's time to reexamine God's command to "turn the other cheek" The context of this passage (Luke 6:27-36) is the command to love our enemies, giving them the benefit of the doubt. God calls us to be forgiving and trusting, but he doesn't want us to be exploited. Just as believers are called to higher standards than non-believers, our friends should be held to higher standards than our enemies.

becoming

Jesus was given
to die for our sins,
and he was raised
from the dead to
make us right
with God.

Cash Flow

Financial problems create a lot of stress, and the Bible has some good advice about how to fix your money problems. First, know the difference between what you want and what you need (Matthew 6:25-34). Second, learn more about money management. Proverbs 20:18 says, "Get advice if you want your plans to work." Finally, remember that "God will use his wonderful riches in Christ Jesus to give you everything you need" (Philippians 4:19).

becoming

becoming

"There are many other things Jesus did. If every one of them were written down, I suppose the whole world would not be big enough for all the books that would be written".

JOHN 21:25

MAY YOUR LIFE BE A BOOK
ABOUT JESUS.

a Bible

that looks like a magazine!

New Century Version
Inside Your Guy's Mind
Interactive quizzes
Relationship Columns
Beauty Becomes Her
What's the Point?
Hospitality 10-1
Health & Fitness
Places to Go, People to See
Women Defined
Calendars
Soulful Meditations
What's Old, What's New?
Money and Wealth
Balancing Act
Recipes
and more...

Becoming is the complete New Testament, but it wouldn't be a culture 'zine if it didn't also address men, beauty, fitness, and food! It's full of applicable ways to integrate faith into your daily life. Becoming gives advice on how to tackle some of life's biggest concerns while taking on some of those not-so-easy-to-understand concepts in the Bible.

www.thomasnelson.c

NCV